The fist of remembering

The fist of remembering

Jim Nason

Dear Mary,

One of the most tender moments for me was that journey from the church to burial sight – As Always you are an Amazing woman!

Jim

Wolsak and Wynn . Toronto

© Jim Nason, 2006

No part of this publication may be reproduced, stored in a retrieval system or transmitted, in any form or by any means, without the prior written consent of the publisher or a licence from The Canadian Copyright Licensing Agency (Access Copyright). For an Access Copyright licence, visit www.accesscopyright.ca or call toll free to 1-800-893-5777.

Cover image: Portrait #1, *Attila Richard Lukacs*
Author's photograph: David Jang
Typeset in Ariel Narrow, printed by The Coach House Printing Company, Toronto, Ontario

"Andrew" and "Bed" appeared in *ARC 53*,Winter 2004.

The publishers gratefully acknowledge
the support of the Canada Council for the
Arts, the Ontario Arts Council, and the Book
Publishing Industry Development Program
(BPIDP) for their financial assistance.

Wolsak and Wynn Publishers Ltd
196 Spadina Avenue, Suite 303
Toronto, ON
Canada M5T 2C2
www.wolsakandwynn.ca

 Canadian   Patrimoine
Heritage   canadien

Library and Archives Canada Cataloguing in Publication

Nason, Jim
         The fist of remembering / Jim Nason.

Poems.
ISBN 1-894987-07-01

         1. Grief — Poetry. 2. Death — Poetry. 3. Cancer — Poetry.
I. Title.

PS8577.A74F57 2006   C811'.54   C2006-900660-1

This book is dedicated to Andrew Thomas Hamilton, 1960 – 2000; and to Kathleen Betty Gray, 1931 – 2004.

Contents

I. SPRING

Spring / 13

II. THE FIST OF REMEMBERING

Andrew / 17
Early evening / 18
All night together / 19
Bed / 20
Pulse / 21
Kiss / 22
The argument / 23
The fist of remembering / 24
Flowers / 25
Fire / 26
Catholicism / 27
The psychic / 28
Steam / 29
Rain / 31
Good love's warm throat / 32
Pause / 33
Spinning / 34
At Boston Harbour / 35
A set of blue eyes on a plate / 36
A black car came humming past / 37
Breakfast / 38
Frost-on-the-car mornings / 39
The canna lily / 40
My dream of medusa as Miss September / 41
Breeze / 42
Saints / 43

III. April

Your hands wooden like a prayer / 47

Life when you left went on with a mind of its own
and on at least one occasion I wished it hadn't / 48

No surprise, you've been transformed into a saint / 49

If I were to make a book for you, I would start with a cut-out,
a silhouette of April – her flowers, her hair / 50

All of memory through a hole in the fence / 51

I can't read your face, but if I had to guess
I'd leave the room for fear of judgement / 52

An aura of words and gold,
Two and a half feet from the chair / 53

I'll put water on for pasta – maybe a peppercorn cream sauce?
And although I may experiment with cooking while naked,
I'll be careful of heat and steam
of appendages too close to the flame / 54

The red tulip had split open
and exposed its blackened wings / 55

Once while hanging curtains in the bay window,
we shined the glass with vinegar and kisses / 56

But could I ever find fire
congruent with the lip of her flame / 57

This is the good flaw of flesh, seed and taste
of sea on the roof of my mouth / 58

Consumed by fire in April,
we made love standing / 59

What do you think about April from over there?
Should I be communing with you and god
over a simple breakfast of water and dry toast? / 60

Add layers of soft to my greying hair? / 61

Remember how we used to kiss
when all that was left was the jagged tremble
of breathing? / 62

"How did I get this?" you'd ask,
looking up. "What happened?" / 63

I discovered stone I never knew existed,
lifted perception's heavy veil / 64

On the peripheral, you are still here – tall, slim, bent over me / 65

It looked more like a poppy folded out,
a stain of yellow on black / 66

Not that it didn't bring me a decent bouquet,
I just didn't have the heart to give her due attention / 67

Let's try to forgive April,
she only wanted to help me sort through
the various heaps and piles of laundry / 68

Make way for a beam of light / 69

Have a look, you said:
This is what brought us close to the window / 70

Delivered in April, the ink smell of cancer,
sores like tongues on your chin / 71

Out from under the gauze of morphine
the occasional gasp of disbelief / 72

Memory is relentlessly slow. Tomorrow
will be flowers, kisses to your marble side / 73

In piles on the kitchen floor / 74

IV. Sunday Evening

Sunday evening / 77

V. Still life

Still life / 81

Acknowledgements / 95

I
SPRING

Spring

The sun is bone white.
A squeegee kid strips off his shirt, thin flesh and muscle-chested.
The black minivan he approaches has enough salt for seven winters.
People seem happy. June in March.
My coat opens like a smile, gives and takes the breeze.
At the top of one grooved and gabled building a man drops
himself with hammer and nail
across the black slate of steep roofing.
Spring repairs early.

There aren't many others. The rusty brick walls of Spadina are warm.
I walk the snake and concrete through the canyon of the city,
the path of high-rises, line of buildings dark and light
that stand still and tall, while the world and I keep moving.

Sprung from the good earth, soon you'll strut and sway
through the double doors of this building.
Helmet in hand, trip over your lovely size ten feet.

II

THE FIST OF REMEMBERING

Andrew

Each day new lumps, hard as pearls spring like bulbs
in staggered rows between the narrow caves of your ribs.
Each day new pain, bone pain. You moan, talk to yourself,

arms and hands float (like ghosts) away from your sides.
From the air above your face you pluck imaginary feathers,
pick apples from high branches, reach through the dark

for the light above our bed. I wanted to touch your alive skin.
Even the tumour that came forth like a Biblical prediction
turned upon one of God's best. Laughing and screaming

it came forth and the rest of you caved in around it.
There wasn't a kiss I could give or a squeeze of hand that could hold you
in this house, that bed, our room. Glass dropper against your teeth,

under your tongue, morphine, lorazapam. You go into yourself inch
by inch. Pound by pound. And your teeth come forward
as do your cheek and skull bones, and your eyes asking

What happened? How did I get like this?
The last week we slept holding hands, yours cold and thin.
Your eyes, two slits of light unspoken. And me, every eight

or ten minutes, I watch the rise and fall of your chest.

Early evening

Things slow down for us. Television, nod-reading,
sleeping, not much need for food. In bed next to you,
I reach through the dark, feel for the heat of your ribs.

I know of course that you are dying.
Figure if I wake you from your morphine slumber
you may stay longer. If I hold the kiss, inhale

as if you are my last kiss and breath, your lips
will stay soft, face less skeletal.

We'll have breakfast by candlelight,
the sun rising instead.

All night together

Our bicycles locked tightly around a shivering maple;
salt, rust, rain, each black frame covered in winter's storm-shadow.

You put your helmet on, smile a big-eyed smile, we ride into morning –
past boxy wire-fence lawns of last year's gardens; stick and flagstone path

of a small person. Sun's sharp shadow on vegetable, herb,
flower skeleton. We talk as we pedal north. Why poverty?

Why so many hateful interpretations of Religion?
Folded in upon themselves, why do buds bother to open?

Bed

We wait for snow and it doesn't come.
All of December it rains.

Toronto, fat city near a filthy lake, has never been taller,
more bouncing with people, condos, and wonderfully foreign dirty movies.

Streetcar by our window. The glass rattles twice.
We go back to white sheets still warm, stay there all afternoon.

Listen to truck and children noises, smell rotten bok-choy,
ten-for-a-dollar Chinatown oranges. We move closer.

Two years. Tops. The oncologist said.
We stared at the negative: two blocks of shadow on a sheet of snow.

Pulse

The lights go out and darkness
settles like an apron
under and through us.
Under bone and bone marrow
your heart refuses to stop until I leave the room.

Kiss

A body cold is different.
Touch someone when he is alive.
Touch him again when he is dead.
Look at the bloodless nose.
Have the courage to kiss him
on the lips.

The argument

Stillness sets in quickly. When they come with the white sheet
you have already dug deep into death. Heels blue, arms

and chest hard. They turn you, like a cardboard image
of yourself, onto the stretcher. All is stiff. Your father

stands near your head. My brother and your brother
sit. Your mother in the corner, arms folded

across her chest. At the foot of the bed,
with God I'm having words.

The fist of remembering

Death takes what it wants.
A square of greed ready for more.
Rich like a pudding, strong on its own sour milk.
And like smoke
it can make my eyes water
and I think twice
about going in for a second look.

You are dead. Not blissful. Not at rest.
Not a rippled column of white
or the smell of vanilla hanging in the room.
Those triceps are ashes.
The bills pile up.
Mail still comes with your name on it.

In the fist, I wait.
I do not turn on the lamp or walk
through the room where you died,
where your heart stopped
and your breathing.
Where your mother tells others
her son came to rest.

Flowers

The light diffuses, a water barrel overflows,
I place my hand into the feel of it. The lovely cold.
Wetness this good should never be taken for granted.

I have heard from the ones brave enough to come
what it was like for them in the days before
and the weeks
and the minutes.
One person brought a bouquet of Monk's Hood –
each purple flower its own hiding.
Death takes on a unique hue.
For some it's the red hot of tulips, for others the blue
of purple articulated by the dab and stroke
of the melancholy artist's portrait,
or the blackness of space
behind an unlit church candle.

Fire

Death is not a dream for those soft at the edge; a caged dog
asking to get out has no manners. And if you're lucky
you'll get a few warts of sun in the middle.
Tap tap tap. Everyone dies with secrets.
I roll out of bed and walk down the stairs to the bathroom. The toilet
faces the mirror. I sit and look at my black hair sticking up in horns, my
                                                                               goatee
a long point. Dark skin puffy, blue eyes burn – my Baptist aunt used to
                                                                                              say,
Evil lives to be ninety, the good die young.

I assumed that once I came further into my waking
the image would go away. Eyes would soften, fire sizzle and cease.
The sun tried to rise, but didn't. I stare at myself and wonder
what has become of me in the weeks since you died. How far the falling?
in which shallow creek will I find water cool enough
to quench and wake me from this spastic sleep?
Wrapped in the fist, I wait with round shoulders, elongated teeth,
pull at my brain for the memory of salt and sweat, your fingers
in places my aunt said boys and men should never be.

Catholicism

We learn, hate everything with horns and hooves.
Burn incense in the dark afternoon by the blue of the Virgin's halo.

A whiskered man's light shines through the weave and eye of the iron grid.
He plays with his collar and beads, heavy strings of diamonds and pearls.
There is breathing.
And breathing that hurts.

I'm in front of the others. Grade two.
Sister Concellia says they should see what a good strapping looks like.
I hold out my hand.
She is coy and beautiful, has light
in the sockets where her eyes belong.
My knees shake and cry without me.

School is a series of months and weeks, small hot hands
pressed and pointed to God. He sits in peace
and safety, never lifts a lace of his finger.

The psychic

Steam and mechanics. Ask the problem a question.
The psychic on Larry King Live says that the dead are all thirty
And happy and that God is a he and she.
She takes calls from people wondering about their deceased.
Are they watching?
Do they hurt?
Do they love and miss me?

The psychic calls everyone Hon, says she sleeps
With the night light on, bedroom full of ghosts.
I want to ask her:
Why is he still here?
What is that tap tap tap on my window?

Steam

What did I do before death came dancing,
dropped these streams of seaweed and mud

across my otherwise dry bed! You said
your triceps were your best muscle

and that you loved the feel of working out.
The pump and stretch of arm and chest,

tight muscles clenched, legs massively spread.
It's the ribs I would go for. The strength of bone

and curve of flesh closest to your heart.
Warm from a day of work. Weeks and months

at the gym. Soft and hard as a sand ripple.
For balance, your back pressed into the bench

and your legs grumbling with the strain
like that protracted second when moans

are hardness joyously shot, broken like a million
droplets of tension and fire on their way
to a Cirque du Soleil swing and juggle extravaganza.
You in the shower. The smell of cranberry soap,

Your perpetual hum like Glenn Gould, only taller.
Not to be wasted heat and water, steam needs to be drunk

and nurtured, cupped and loved like a lap dancer
bent over a table. And I laugh and dare say

pass the soap. Be careful of water. Of overflow.
we are notorious now and to blame

for the leaks in the ceiling.
Our tenants listen below.

Rain

This mirror is not a mirror, table, a picture hung crooked on the wall.
The plant in the north window will always be green and growing,
heavy and lopsided with your ghost-head. The water
in the barrel continues its overflow. And yes, like a predictable cliché, rain
like the tap tap tap of Rilke against my window.

Good love's warm throat

The poor have their own language. When they are angry
you know whathefucksgoingonintheirmouth
and it might be a handful of black half-teeth falling out
or a tongue pointed like a sting.
I have brought being alone to an affective grace.
No red silk.
Now white light.
Alone in the dark, the halo of *Jerry Springer*
on my screen-stunned face.

Me and my t.v. don't answer the phone. When people walk by on the street
with dogs or other people, I close the blinds, hold my breath, don't laugh
at the cousin having an affair with her sister's husband.
The light is still out
and why should anyone know what keeps me
from the well meant mouth of conversation,
good love's warm throat.

Pause

Unprovoked, a bubble forms between my lips.
Smaller than an egg.
Bigger than a pea.
A roll of glass, there like an answer;
I swallowed without listening to what it might have said.

Spinning

I sit in the coffee shop during the day, read and write. A man in black coat,
Black cap, grey hair and eye glasses sits next to me. Go away,
I think. You remind me of men who take up too much space,
Small neon rooms with pompous ceilings.
People with bad teeth.
Everything I hate.

My brain makes circles of light. My feet want to leave the city.
Now I'm spinning, flying geography.

At Boston Harbour

Seagulls fight over a half donut, orange peel, fries.

Air is salty with heat. Cambridge boys flex in the sun, show muscled chest,
pumped-up arms, and thick-like-love ready-to-go legs.
Oh to be mighty with sun and sky
and to have plenty of good questions!

The tide comes in at an angle.
Ride and tide, upswing of wave, the sun turns itself
over and over again.
I am pushed gently along the beach. Spitting salt and water.
I'm glad for the ocean, for the sand and dunes, the relentlessly sexy heat.
For the clarity of noontime light, the rocks smoothed by salt, ocean
and other rocks pushing and pulling for eternity.

The trip home on the *Rapid-Ferry* speeding over blue.
White and light, a rush of air
where your breathing should be.

A set of blue eyes on a plate

Outrageous brew, this coffee is something else. Boston has its fair share
of beans, sunshine and well-worn cobblestones.
Nice pie-slice blocks, old and new buildings
glassed and framed meticulously.
Police officers are perfectly overweight. Italian men
in the village eat decent spoons of gelato
while the wives get stoned on rapid-fire talk,
abundantly hot and sugared drinks.

I find a church and talk with Joseph and St. Francis,
St. Lucy in amber, pink and red. She holds a set of blue eyes
on a plate. The martyred saint of sight.
Dante's guide.
Divine siren, she calls.
Her eyes follow me from the plate:
glowing pyramid of truth,
brilliant wink of light.

I want that plate for my collection.

A black car came humming past

Limp, lengthy, fragrant, morning comes as mist. *Angel's Trumpets* fold in like keenly rolled napkins. The lane behind the garden crawls with crack dealers, hookers, and heroin in blood-stained needles.
Good life, night life.
Nakedness.
Closeness and dirt.

This summer past I managed a muscle reconfiguration and a suntan, enough rain, lilies, and heat to start my own Jesus station. I sat in a hotel room, a black car came humming past every eight or seven seconds.

Imagine a corpse in your bed.
I want out of this.

Breakfast

If you're going to walk tall, walk big.
Toast is burning
and I am Proust somewhere in the fist of remembering.
Kiss and taste you in the morning.
Peaches and oatmeal, toasted sunflower seed.
Grief like skin in the apple of my teeth.

Frost-on-the-car mornings

My house is in order, the plants put to rest,
mornings require a simple black sweater.

What is left of me needs to be muscle.
The drive to work is fresh and at certain intersections
painfully bright. Cars brake quickly.
One cyclist slides between my squint
and the glass of the Hydro building.
The first hint of fall. Of falling leaves,
frost-on-the-car mornings.
Of abundant apples and squash.
all things orange, ripe or red from weeks and months of sunning.

I have managed summer.
Provincetown is sexy.
New York moves like a vibrant snake.
Toronto opens her fine highways and the *International Film Festival*
makes for plenty of finger flickering in the dark and hands greased
where popcorn should be. And good buildings grow straight
while others not so lucky fade, crumble with grace,
covered in the green-tea smell of Chinatown.

The nervous drive east. Try not to read into the longer shadow
of passing cars. What is coming will come.
The Westbound streetcar.
Night falling from me.

The canna lily

She waits until September to show her shoulders. Splintered and bent, like Katherine Hepburn, she won't have anything to do with pretend flowers. I've had a headache for days. Someone needs to clean the dirt and violence left by raccoons and squirrels. They do what they want, unfed children on a muddy plane.

When mist from the garden hose touches two morning glories they unfold like a slow-motion *National Geographic* sequence.
Canna lily, bent over, laughing.
A wasp about my feet like a drunk
saturated in the tired poison of being kicked out.

My dream of medusa as Miss September

White bread is something to eat with butter, and heaps of steaming
                                                                spaghetti
are likely to come wet and snaking into my dream of Medusa as Miss
                                                                September.
No one can prepare you. I dream.
He is goodness dead.
He still has size ten feet.
Only now they are confident. Not bruised.
Only one is tripping.

Breeze

October is here with passion and colour
usually reserved for born-again flowers. Burning trees.
He walks in sandals through the sway and rustle of me.
Leaves and sun blend into warm folds of fall.
I walk in circles, around city blocks.
Victorian homes on Sullivan Street, condos on Phoebe.

A breeze through the trees like waves of yellow morning
brazen flower pushing me before I have eaten my full fit of grief.
I water plants, plant other plants, wash the car.
Eyes closed, sit for an hour with the sun on my face.
Clouds cross over – I know this by the presence
or absence of heat.

Saints

I am pleased about time and what it has done. A desk could be a pencil,
a pencil is something to be careful about.
Like Greta Garbo, I don't need excuses for a tear
in my bathrobe. Drops of dream like pellets, the sky
vivid as chrome, stars fall.
Only I'm not so beautiful as needle peaks.
My body is made of glass and stone.
Tall. Boxed. Radiating heat.

Muscular saints work out four times a week at *Bally's Fitness*
and each perfect body has its own cocky smile
reserved for moments when towels, double-draped, drop
below washboard-hard-waist
a lively spot for the tent-pole-of-love to flower,
find someone of comparable endurance,
over-the-top good taste.

*

Home. In bed. The phantom-head of fan oscillating,
its shadow rolling slowly from side to side.
I keep one pillow under my head,
one between my legs,
a third for company.

Humidity drips off the window
like grease and steam.
The city grows in clusters
and clusters of city.
Citycore Condo Complex
has blocked my view of the lake.

No matter. I like brick
and the feel of brick.
Morning will come
with bird and car sounds,
hammer and scaffolding.
Tap tap tap.
A stretch of warmth
on my eyes and chin.
Take me carefully
to the blue behind the screen.

III

APRIL

Your hands wooden like a prayer

Get dressed for April, she does not feel like June.
Billie Holiday trembles, the coffee maker spits
and sprays. The anticipation is about rain.
Breeding, mixing, stirring.
Unmannered erections,
T. S. Eliot on the table.

Help me with the yellow in my stomach
and the scrambled eggs. You know
cars travel fast outside the window and birds slide
and spin, spring is more than the sea foam of love,
the gradual undoing of ice and wind.

Melting snow has just reached the worm.
Rain like Rilke, the tap tap tap
on my window.

**Life when you left went on with a mind of its own
and on at least one occasion I wished it hadn't**

Some days are plenty of birds chirping.
A child in the schoolyard.
The sky lonely as a fence.

Think of the fist now unclenched,
shampoo smell of morning
like a kiss on your head.
Memory has made its revisions.

Who can deny the appeal of wine and maybe cigarettes,
of perfume and hairspray?
And some mornings
sour and drunk,
April smells as if love
has been on her all night.

**No surprise, you've been transformed
into a saint**

And I'm jealous of your status on top – calm, wise,
and why the brown robe? I was led to believe that Heaven
was all done up in beige, ivory, and muted earth tones.

The Angel of Revelation's feet are on fire. I have tasted spring water.
Sometimes April is a bleeding-heart hanging from a fine green stem.

Praying to God is a one-sided fence. Today I am falling,
tomorrow I will fly.

**If I were to make a book for you, I would start with a cut-out,
a silhouette of April – her flowers, her hair**

Mere shadow of his former self, night
like a charcoal smudge across the sky.

In the morning me and the sun
race to the pink lip of the horizon.

All of memory through a hole in the fence

Certain routines are more difficult than others.
The alarm sounded but I didn't wake.
      Take it in, give it back.
      That's the nature of sex.

April is warmer than usual.
I must and shall do the laundry,
it's full of want and expectation.

Always, April.

She left me a note on the dryer door
      meet me at the Sky Dome, under the gargoyle

**I can't read your face, but if I had to guess
I'd leave the room for fear of judgement**

I take an oath with you. Kiss your eyes
while you sleep, run my fingers along
the pink horizon of your lips, cover you
with endless brush strokes of finger.

And like a decent painter, the colour sings
and flows. I keep the essence of my promise and fall
on the curve of your hip with kisses

down to your inner thigh,
lick and taste the ring of your finger.
Sour with salt and sea milk, you ask,
is ambisexual a word?

An aura of words and gold,
Two and a half feet from the chair

Today is oranges with sunflower seeds
toasted in cinnamon, a milky coat,
skin thin as the skin of an egg soft boiled.

Unbutton the day, unbutton my pants,
unbutton the link in the chain. Her kissing technique
should not be taken lightly. I still taste her in the morning.
My lips carry her electricity.

**I'll put water on for pasta – maybe a peppercorn cream sauce?
And although I may experiment with cooking while naked,
I'll be careful of heat and steam
of appendages too close to the flame**

I should be asleep but am awake. With you, kissing
'til the cows come home can hurt.

Lips were not designated for such freedom and friction.
If I'm going to read, going to read a language, I must and shall
the sky read.

Born of heat, born of April, outside began to spit
at our window. Spit. Outside spat at our window, spit.

The moon was almost full against the blue-black night.
The horizon was orange. The miracle of unfolding,
we tore one another apart.

Lean towards the window she begged, and I did.
She pulled me by my hip flexor back to bed
for another week of nights.

The red tulip had split open
and exposed its blackened wings

The children wanted to start a fire, and had the good manners
to ask for matches. It was all innocent – the digging of the circle,
the ring of stone and brick, and although they appeared
somewhat dry, there was no outward sign
that the trees would burst into flame.

Instead, a walk to the lake was declared. The cliffs and pebbles
had had it with winter. April asked me for my hand – let's go to New York,
                                                                she said.
The children skipped stones on the water and skipped. Let's go alone,
she whispered, slid her hand into my pocket.

**Once while hanging curtains in the bay window,
we shined the glass with vinegar and kisses**

If love is an invitation, lets take our pants off.
Now is the time to roll up your sleeves.
My watch must be broken, everything seems to have stopped
from the minute I tasted the soil
on the nail of your index finger,
washed it about my dirty mouth.

The sun straight overhead tells me
in ten minutes it will be time for soup
and grilled cheese. On Queen Street
there are cafeterias that serve a large dill pickle
with your tuna melt or egg salad.

Grownups should not stay in bed
too long, lick the crumbs off their knees.

April straddles May
like a teenager
over her father's *Penthouse* magazine.

But could I ever find fire
congruent with the lip of her flame

Clarity like a flame in the window, the sun arrives
with a bundle of birds for the roof.
The maple tree is latent with syrup, lilies, and the lilacs
have performed their fragrant sex act. A single drop of flood,
April shows her legs. Ask for more – her thighs,
her lips and her lips again – she'll show you an ocean.
Bleeding heart, peony, tiger lily – random acts of colour along the fence.

**This is the good flaw of flesh, seed and taste
of sea on the roof of my mouth**

April
has a way of crawling,
rain falling
hard on her shoulders,
hair in the mud of her throat.

Personification of a season is somewhat risky,
but how could I say no to blue eyes like this,
concentric ring of gold at the centres.

And the grass is screaming to grow.
Seagulls cry the blues.
A tree by the entrance of the schoolyard,
fatter than the sidewalk gate,
branches up into three distinct sections
and sub-sections of grey, and grey-white, sky.

**Consumed by fire in April,
we made love standing**

Nobody needs to know about the tongue business
but I'll tell you anyhow that things went well
and it was a damn healthy push and probe of lip on lip.

Groin against groin, try to stay inside this hopping skin
because you're about to learn about the good stretch
and pull of love if you wish.

Not that I wrote the book, but I'll gladly go on
the tour, get lost in the wind and whistle
of various wet positions.

**What do you think about April from over there?
Should I be communing with you and god
over a simple breakfast of water and dry toast?**

The drop-off point of remembering is at the edge of no person.
Plumb the depths, remember though,
morning is a critical point of inspection.

But be sure to think of the wave,
it's bigger than you imagine – overbearing and black,
wide as the sea that dreams of being an ocean.

Add layers of soft to my greying hair?

Grey smells of winter.

Assembler of words, creator of dew – April
in a strapless dress.
Blossoms from the chestnut fall like rain
and a flood of white rain.

A small puddle of belly below her breasts,
brown nipples of flat stone and fish, blue eyes
big as a Petri dish.

My view of the rain is obstructed by maples.
Tap tap tap on the glass – branches and stems,
twigs through the window.

**Remember how we used to kiss
when all that was left was the jagged tremble
of breathing?**

April carried me away like a limp cliché of myself,
up a winding staircase, dropped me on a bed
with plenty of room for ten,

but we were alone
all week
with our clothes off.

Some days she is seaweed and mud.
Remember the water? she asks.
The perpetual hum and overflow
of stream and babble?

**"How did I get this?" you'd ask,
looking up. "What happened?"**

The dream seems real at first.
April gives her Doberman, Fluffy, a bone
big as a house. I want the bone for myself.
Fluffy's teeth are carved of slate,
held together with barbed wire.

And then the rain. Breathe out.
Fear tightens like a viper
about your throat – strain of vein
around your bulging eyes, legs stiff
as a child's doll.

Breathe out. Breathe out.

Death is never too far from the table.
Crow picks at the blackened sun.
Fluffy snarls when you back away.

**I discovered stone I never knew existed,
lifted perception's heavy veil**

On one occasion
while the door was open
while I was raw of skin
while the curtain weaved and fell,
death crossed over
arm and leg
to my side of the wall.

Blood-red face, skin an orgy of warts,
blue-black eyes like a bruise
a shiny black stone in the middle of each.
Tattooed-on-smile,
he sat on the edge of my bed
filled the room with the ammonia smell of bile.

In his blistered hands
slivered with dirt and scale
he held and caressed my foot

led me to believe
his hands were cupped in prayer
his tongue rough as a cat's
and hot enough to burn.

Rats at the underside of my bed.

On the peripheral, you are still here – tall, slim, bent over me

Red and yellow tulips along the fence.
Black birds and squirrels fight over trash.

The old Chinese woman pushes her top-heavy cart
up the street, past the dirty islands of ice in the shade
of the Spadina building. Crates of oranges, broccoli, ginger root,
a bank tower on each dirty corner. The promise of blue. Cold wind,
residual dusting of grey.

**It looked more like a poppy folded out,
a stain of yellow on black**

Air-conditioned and clean enough, some places
call us back more than others.

The pot smells like it's burning.
Never let the coffee come to a boil
— April's instructions to the waitress.

Not that it didn't bring me a decent bouquet,
I just didn't have the heart to give her due attention

If evil is a backward movement away from good,
the sun better think over its spin.
The support workers are on strike,
trash blows and builds
with rats and rat castles
along the brick and wall of the school.
Good morning, says April,
leaning across the fence.

**Let's try to forgive April,
she only wanted to help me sort through
the various heaps and piles of laundry**

April says we should take a drive while the weather is sunny
and find a meadow somewhere surrounded by cows and trees,
and make love in the grass while cows chew their cud and cream

their cream in envy as we fall on top of newly fallen leaves.
The body remembers, feels hot.
Fingers are branches growing out.
The fist, a mass of blood and blood
held against someone else.

Death is an acute lack of circulation.

Make way for a beam of light

Backwards down a slippery slope
and the brakes wouldn't work on the car.
I switched myself awake.
Longer shiver of skin, morning unravels
like a good peel of apple.

Strawberries, delphinium, peony in clusters.
Tap tap tap. Always, April.

Have a look, you said:
This is what brought us close to the window

I dream a tornado is twisting and rearranging two stanzas,
one line,
and eleven vowels
of a twenty-eight-stanza poem
and April hands me a glass of orange juice
and a one-page letter written with the ink of a silver pen.

She is pregnant again and milk gathers
beneath the cracks and tips
of her nipples.
Foam and sea foam hang about the lip of the ocean.
All is wave and tide.
What gets left at the seashore is edible.
Sometimes I put seaweed on my tuna melt,
clams on spinach and pasta,
salt and salt of ocean on my tongue.

**Delivered in April, the ink smell of cancer,
sores like tongues on your chin**

The eyelid is a delicate muscle, thinner than the skin of a grape,
in my sleep it holds back the eye of the dream.

All cars have a red sparkle, that's the way it is in the downpour of rain.
The dam will turn the highway into a lake: gallons and a million gallons
of silver-grey.

Afternoon sun causes steam against the flat blue sky.
Slip another wool over my eye, another brilliant dream.

**Out from under the gauze of morphine
the occasional gasp of disbelief**

Spring is a walk into longer days and into the green.
Each day in succession, we worked hard
to get our feelings on paper.

There wasn't a dry tear in the house.
A woman's water breaks in the middle
of a department store, a brilliant rush flows from her
like a flood of children to the floor.

A car backs over a bicycle.
A child has a nosebleed, uses his shirt as a blotter,
red ink drops of blood gather and merge.

April turns blue as ice.

**Memory is relentlessly slow. Tomorrow
will be flowers, kisses to your marble side**

My view of downtown is blocked more and more
each minute by green and by buildings.
Daffodils and tulips proud but still.

I slept each night with one eye opened to the stars.
Hibiscus gather in clusters while summer
falls through April.

Don't fuss so much with morning, she says,
with a big throat yell.
The birds concur. Whistle. Pause. Whistle.

Breeze through the trees. Silence.

A fold of monarch butterflies, dandelions, and sunshine
like a knife. Under my chin, April.
April.
And more April on my lips,
but a sadness.

In piles on the kitchen floor

The storm converged
on the horizon
broke off into several twisters.
Black and tightening at the base –
each funnel hissing,
like a bag of cobras.
We put our heads to the ground

and put them together.
And before we could finish our thought
we were carried across the horizon
like crows. The sun came burning out.

Our shadow stretched as a trench
of darkness across the ground.
The sky is black and wide.
And from our flight across the sky,
our wings flapping like legs,
thoughts like two birds.

And then I jumped from my dream, head split
at the foot of the bed – April had removed the glass
from the window, a rush of air tickled the raw
of my newly cut brain.

The first pinprick of night – ah! stars.

IV

Sunday Evening

Sunday evening

The kitchen is the last place I expected to find you.
In two orange lights – one by the stove, the other

against the north wall. But it was more than the light
split in two. It was the feeling of light in the room

and then inside me. It was the way my entire
body danced inside out but I did not move

and my scalp tingled and rushed like a wave
pulsing to join the room. Then my brain kicked in,

trying to figure it all out, asking for more – for proof
– for a voice, for something concretely visual

like a corporate logo or something only you and I knew.
And all the while the flesh above my cheek bones

and around my mouth tingled. *Ah!* said my brain.
This dancing on my roof, this lightness and light,

has to do with the temperature. Close the door.
Shut the window. Leave the room!

But I was not hot. I was not cold.
And the rushing continued to my groin

and back up to my throat.

V
STILL LIFE

Still life

       i.
Three years since your death
and I'm still staring down
my memory of you
in the casket.

Knew the colouring would be all wrong
and the clothing navy and stiff. Knew
there would be lots of flowers
and concern about those flowers
and whose flowers

would go where.

Knew I would be frightened
by the sight of you
not moving.

Realised every inch of us
rushes to rescue someone we love
when he is not breathing.

      ii.
An undertaker should
employ the best make-up artist
to do justice to life in the dead,

a match on its way
to the bigger flame of the candle.
I am that artist.

iii.

There is a slit under your chin
and along your wrist. I understand
that embalming had to take place.
Still, I can't look

                          (rather, I look,
                  but through a gauze
                   like a photograph –
                     a quick click ,
                 grayish negative
                       of the day.
                    I walk and talk,
                  hold my breath
between appreciative nods
                      of my head –
                then again, it isn't
           a photograph, it's a film
          like the black-and-white
                        sections
                       of a train
              moving, while you
                        lie still
                    at the station)

at you
in your mid-price casket.

Children chasing one another
through empty pews
where row upon row
of people will quietly sit.

The children screaming
with delight when we rearrange
the casket so that your head
will face west
rather than east.

The lower half of you
in the closed part – shoes on or off?
Trousers and socks?

Whatever I imagine or guess
is not the you I want.

I turn to the corner
behind the casket – dark
with faint flicker of candle.
The usual terracotta walls
shine unsteadily with shadow,
project an offspring of fear.

      iv.
Draw the outline of the subject in position.
You may do an underdrawing.
Be conscious of figure and shadow;
your subject vertical,
now horizontal.

Gradually deepen colours.
The challenge is to bear in mind
the rapport between the piece you are working on
and the completed picture, you outside looking in.
A mirage-like halo of light around your subject.
Wet on wet, glazes and impasto;
contrast and harmony, rhythm and movement;
and perspective ….
There are many ways to approach your subject;
however, you must prepare to let go
of the notion that it is possible
to get it perfect
but never stop
trying
to get light
just right
in the face of the dead.

      v.
Photograph of us.
I kiss the cold glass
as I do most nights.

Close my eyes
and there you are –
hands folded in the casket,
strong-bone grey.

How to recall the strength of you?

vi.
I want undetectable gradations
of pink in your cheeks
like a healthy man –
with a pinch of life
and the tan you always had
from biking up and down city streets.

All year round you rode
with groceries and books,
flowers sticking out of the brown pannier
like tulips and daisies alive
in the earth.

vii.
Bound to you through time in niche number 407,
0.032 cubic metres. You questioned my decision
to share the space – "But there may be another?"
(more a sad plea than a statement).

But there was no doubt in my mind.
I couldn't imagine sharing this box
with anyone else –
0.032 cubic metres of us,
two souls side-by-side
off at night
while the alive sleep –
laughing and flying through
stars.

A blank space below your name
for mine.

     viii.

Rilke says all is gestation
and then bringing forth. That January blizzard
you brought me an enormous bouquet of white flowers,
coffee, a *Globe & Mail* on your bike? I stood there
wondering how you balanced
through the snow! Do you remember
I kissed your cold cheek,
shook the snow from your coat.
When you left
that morning
I was happy
in the knot of my throat
in the light of a blizzard
as I opened the door
to wind and blowing snow.

Our first kiss
was awkward,
we couldn't get the lips
just right.

ix.
At the sleep disorder centre
the clinician connects wires
to my heart
brain and jaw
and under eyes
to test the flutter of my dreams.
        Do I snore and gasp? she asks.
        Suddenly bolt and scream?

Get into itchy pyjamas (haven't worn for years),
slide under beige duvet, careful not to pull out wires.
Aware of camera overhead,
traffic on Bathurst street,
dirty carpet,
the room small
as a bathhouse cubicle.

Had a dream I was spreading seeds randomly
over freshly cut lawn. Although tulips come
from bulbs, these were tulip seeds,
thousands of them, I scattered
over valleys and men. I ran up
and down trying to imagine
spring, my hand
in the grainy bag,
digging and pulling
clumps of coloured seeds.

I wonder how images look
on an electroencephalogram.
Wonder what they've seen.

And you? Clearly the otherworld
must be one step closer to dreams.

    x.
Leaving your body
like leaving a too-tight shoe,
the soul off to someplace
far more expansive.

Canon Beach, hill-size boulders
in the sand. Us laughing,
endlessly lapping shores
of light and autumn.
How to create a beach –
flecks of grey
overlay of brown,
brush of red
where sand is wet,
white where you want the sun
to shine down on water –
sky and earth reversed.

    xi.
The glass over this photograph (wet
with cold and kisses).
We look happy.

Life, like a good painting,
is meant to breathe –
oranges, grapes, fruit sliced open
should cause one to salivate,
to taste and crave
the juice of an overripe pear
split in two, lungs
expanding and dancing
in your chest.
And there should be a hovering
over your body, a ripple of light
blatant as Jesus' walk on water,
subtle as the smile on your face
when our feet touched
under the table
at your parents' house.

xii.
What if a funeral
were more like a baptism
with abundant water for schools
of fish, plenty of light
and music
to guide them up the river?

Too abrupt, this scene in the casket.
Too unnaturally still. Too many
sad strangers in one place.
This bad attempt at imitating life
I suppose is proof enough
something irreversible has come about.

But the stitches in your mouth?
At the very least the threads
should not show.

I want your lips full,
a little moisture –
more alive with red.
And how can I make you smile?
A smile, I know, must seem over-the-top
for the dead – but it's a smile
that causes eyes
to sparkle, your eyes
now closed.

    xiii.
You in a casket, us in a photo,
me on the loop heading north,
cinnamon bun on my briefcase,
knotted twists of sugar and dough – digression
from my usual bland muffin.
I've learned, go south first
and you'll get a seat
when the train empties at
Union Station.

But it's more than that,
it's the stalling, putting off the day
for another four or six minutes.

It's the holding on
to the train,
the men and women
with fresh hair, shiny shoes, briefcases,
too much cologne or perfume.
It's the legs and arms next to me
as we rumble under the towers at King.
Train shakes the woman
not able to get a seat –
dropping the book
she reads while standing;
man with briefcase next to me
gazes out the window,
his leg inching closer
and I catch his reflection
looking back at me
when the train flashes
along the platform
at St. Clair.
Don't leave, I want to say.
But when he goes
I'm secretly glad,
put my hand where he was,
warm and creased and willing.
The train rumbles forward.
More people on than off.

> *– For you created my in-most parts;*
> *You knit me together in my mother's womb. –*
>
> *Psalm 139*

If paintings, like poems,
are never finished, only set aside,
how then do I decide which colour
to leave last on the page – red
of the roses brought by friends?
White of the satin lining of the casket?
Blue of your eyes?

Night time. Our first
kiss. Awkward.
Couldn't
get
the lips
just
right.

But we keep trying that moment over
and over. Time together
determined by light.

You on satin.
But it is not you, only the flesh
of you. How to paint your kick
and slide through the womb (it too like a too-tight shoe)
under the bright lights of delivery. Your mother

says she heard angels singing
someone brought a warm cloth
for the midwife's hands –
she used it for your handsome face,
wet and stained with crying
then peace.

XV.

We arrive here through a crap-shoot swim.
Through our mother's adrenaline
and fear. Through blood
of God
and blood
of birth.
And maybe in the walking
we find someone else –
niche 407 without light
but the promise of it.
Red onions,
basil and garlic –
our first kiss
a little awkward,
couldn't get the lips just right –

the sauce burning on the stove.

Acknowledgements

Thanks to the Phoebe-Walmer Collective. To my many teachers, among them John Ashbery, Mark Doty, Don Coles, Don Summerhayes., Paul Lisicky, and Mathew Corigon. To my parents; my extraordinary sister, Siovhon; and to my brothers Bill, Steve, Mike, Ron and Earl. To Maria Jacobs and Noelle Allen. And to Peter Dawson with enormous respect, gratitude and admiration.